The Perfect Place

Written by Lisa Trumbauer
Illustrated by Cheryl Mendenhall

Harcourt Achieve
Rigby • Saxon • Steck-Vaughn

www.HarcourtAchieve.com
1.800.531.5015

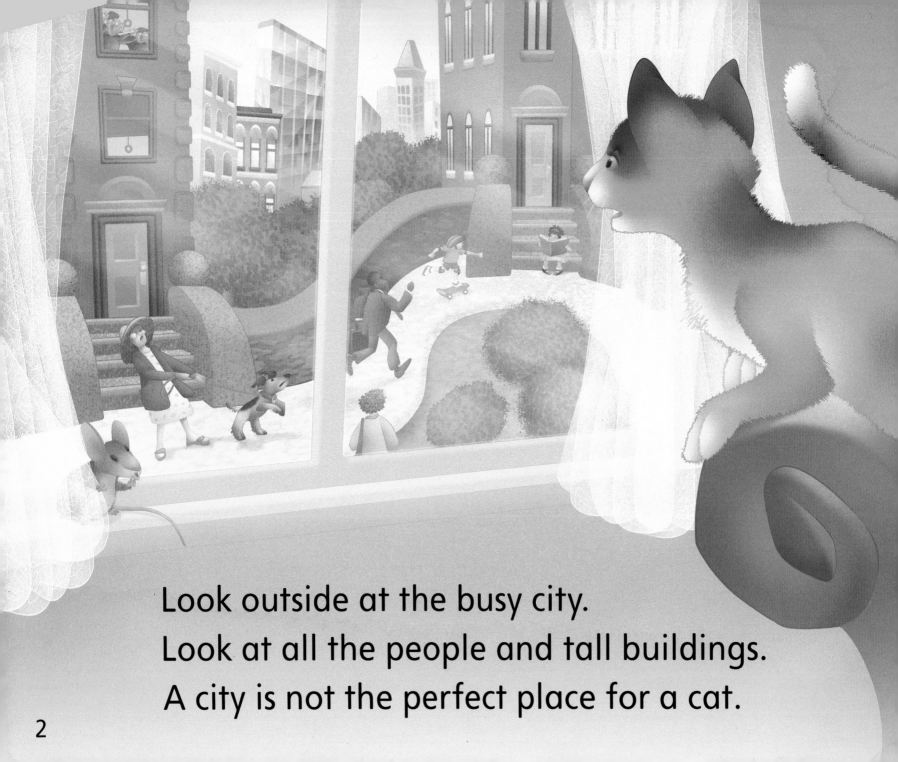

Look outside at the busy city.
Look at all the people and tall buildings.
A city is not the perfect place for a cat.

A forest is the perfect place!
A forest has lots of trees to climb.
A forest has lots of places to sleep.

3

But a forest gets a lot of rain.

Cats don't like rain!

Maybe a forest is not the perfect place.

A desert is the perfect place!
A desert does not get much rain.
A desert is hot and dry.

But a desert has snakes.
Cats don't like snakes!
Maybe a desert is not the perfect place.

The Arctic is the perfect place!
The Arctic does not have snakes.
The Arctic has snow to play in.

7

But the Arctic has polar bears.

Cats don't like polar bears!

Maybe the Arctic is not the perfect place.

Maybe the perfect place is right here!
Yes, a city is the perfect place for a cat.

Close
AND
Turn

Glossary

cactus

rattlesnake

kangaroo rat

roadrunner

Some people think nothing can live in the desert.
But there are many desert plants and animals.
For them, the desert is just right!

Close AND Turn

Roadrunners can run very fast.
They rest in the hot part of the day.
Roadrunners eat rattlesnakes!

Rattlesnakes like the desert sun.
They lie on top of rocks on warm days.
Rattlesnakes eat kangaroo rats!

Kangaroo rats hide from the sun in the day.
They come out for food at night.
Kangaroo rats eat seeds and grasses.

In the desert, things live without much water.
This cactus keeps water in its leaves.
Animals eat cactus leaves to get water.

In the desert, there is not much rain.
This desert is hot in the day. It is cold at night.

THE LIVING DESERT

Written by Lisa Trumbauer

Harcourt Achieve

Rigby • Saxon • Steck-Vaughn

www.HarcourtAchieve.com
1.800.531.5015